A Self-Healing Brain:
A Gate to the Soul

Becoming your balance and complete self
by learning how to work with your brain

by

Roya R. Rad

The author's mission is to write pieces that are longer than an article but shorter than a typical book for the busy reader who has a curious and thirsty mind and who seeks the core of the information. She attempts to make her writings up-to-the point, practical, easy to grasp and based on quality not quantity.

BALBOA
PRESS

A DIVISION OF HAY HOUSE

Balboa Press books may be ordered through booksellers or by contacting:

Balboa Press
A Division of Hay House
1663 Liberty Drive
Bloomington, IN 47403
www.balboapress.com
1-(877) 407-4847

Printed in the United States of America.

ISBN: 978-1-4525-7262-8 (sc)
ISBN: 978-1-4525-7263-5 (e)

Balboa Press rev. date: 4/25/2013

Disclaimer
The author makes an effort to give valid information to the public; however, she makes no guarantee with respect to the accuracy or completeness of the contents of the books published. Science is unlimited, and there are many facts yet to be discovered and improved upon. **The author's mission is to write pieces that are longer than an article but shorter than a typical book, she hopes to give her readers a source of information that is full to capacity, up-to-the point, and simple to grasp.**

Dedication

I dedicate this book to all those deep thinkers who are true seekers of spirituality. I also dedicate it to all those who have inspired me one way or the other through their genuine acts or words.

Note to the reader:

As an author, I prefer minimum editorial work on my thought process to make sure the message is communicated as it comes to my thought and as it was intended. In addition, my writing style is focused on putting as much information in as few pages as possible to make it easy for the busy readers of today's world.

Contents

Introduction: A Fully Functioning Brain   ix

Your Brain, Your Happiness, Your Health   1

The Spiritual Brain   7

The Emotional Brain   11

The Rational Brain   17

The Disciplined Brain   21

The Creative Brain   25

The Intuitive Brain   29

A Social Brain   33

A Balanced Brain   39

Last Words   43

Introduction:
A Fully Functioning Brain

A fully functioning human being who is complete and content lives through a fully functional brain. A balanced self has a balanced brain. A complete sense of self is not possible without a brain that is in a state of completeness, equilibrium and stability. A brain that is healthy has a steadiness between its different parts and structures; no one part of it is too heavily or too lightly active. Such a brain has a design that works in harmony with itself and with the person and their surroundings. It is literally impossible to be who you are unless your brain functions properly. Your brain's functionality determines your happiness, how effective you are, how positive you are, how successful you are at passing through life's challenges, what type of a parent you become, how you handle your relationships, and how compassionate you are; it also determines your thought process, including your beliefs, and how you experience pleasure and pain. ***The brain is the hardware of your soul, your essence, and the core of your being.***

The good news is that there is mountain of evidence indicating that many of the skills necessary to have a healthy brain can be attained through training, awareness, knowledge and practice. ***There is an overwhelming amount of evidence indicating that you can change the physiology of your brain and fix many of the problems you suffer from.***

A healthy brain is a logical, intuitive, creative, emotionally mature, intellectually open minded, and a well balanced brain. A rational brain is able to respond to verbal communication, can solve problems logically and systematically, looks at the differences, prefers set rules, has self-control, likes hierarchy, and is a splitter. An intuitive brain responds to visual communication, responds to hunches, looks for patterns, is spontaneous, is comfortable with uncertainty, likes a free internal feeling, thinks collectively, and is holistic and integrative. Furthermore, and to elaborate, there are two main areas to the brain, the right and the left. The right brain is responsible mostly for insight, artistic pursuits, imagination, and awareness. Right brain individuals are more extroverted, are more of a risk taker, look at the big picture and are more creative. Left brain individuals are more logical, focus more on details, plan ahead and are practical. When these two sides of the brain work in harmony and in balance, the brain is working fully.

As you can see, all of these in a moderate form can be healthy, but too much of any one of them may not be as healthy. For example, if you are too logical and are not in tune with your feelings or are not willing to use your intuition, then you may miss half of the picture, and vice-versa. Many of us cannot afford and choose not to live life half-full. We want to experience it fully without any regrets, and in order to do that we need to do what we can to make the brain work for us, not against us. And again, the good news is that we have much control over that.

Your Brain, Your Happiness, Your Health

There are four major areas of the brain that are directly involved with human behavior and psychology. Deep limbic system, basal ganglia, prefrontal cortex and cingulate system. The deep limbic system which is in the center of the brain is related to mood. When off balance, people suffer from moodiness and being negative. Then there is the basal ganglia which is related to the idling speed. When overactive, it creates anxiety, panic, irrational fears, and too much negative attention on little things and avoidance of the real problems of life. Another area of the brain related to human's behavior is the prefrontal cortex. This area is the most advanced area of the brain; it is like a mature, rational and adult side of us who helps us stay focused, have plans, not act impulsively, delay gratification, and make the right decisions.

The overall way of our thinking affects our general state of mind. When the deep limbic system is too active, the mind focuses too much on negative filtration; it makes the person moody, irritable, socially isolated and prone to depression.

To heal the limbic system and the problems associated with it one must focus on rational and truthful thinking, manage and process her memories, use her senses to enjoy small things in life (e.g. smelling pleasant scents stimulates the limbic system positively), and find healthy connections with others. To do that the person must learn to become aware and get rid of automatic negative thought, regular use of words like "always" or "never", "everybody", "nobody", seeing the negative in everything, thinking that one can predict the future and read minds, confusing thinking with feeling, too much guilt, blaming others and not taking responsibility, and taking too many things personally. By teaching yourself to control these thoughts and process the raw emotions, you can change your brain's structure.

Other ways of structuring the brain to heal it includes eating healthy foods and avoiding unhealthy ones. For example, alcohol and drugs have been shown to create holes in the brain and a reduction of cerebral blood flow and cerebral metabolism. We need to have a brain that not only has a healthy cortical function, but also can pay attention and make sense of what we feel and why we feel it. Alcohol can affect the limbic system and as a result the emotional process.

The structure of the brain also changes by the interactions we have and the people we surround ourselves with. It is important to have reparative relationships if we want to heal our brains; healthy relationships with people who bring us awareness, health, kindness, support and positivity. In order to do that, we need to learn skills to attract such people. Healthy people skills enhances limbic bonds. Some of these skills are making effort to make the relationship positive, not taking the good of it for granted, focusing on the positive of it and resolving what seems negative, keeping the relationship exciting, communicating effectively and positively, building trust, running away from difficulties, and making time.

Physical contact like touch, whether in the form of intimate relationships, a hug, a message, or just a simple friendly touch, are all important to the functioning of the brain. Then other things like good natural smells, things that bring good memories, physical activity, connecting with nature, doing something creative, and helping other people, are all essential to the healing of the brain.

Another important factor to the brain healing process is learning to forgive and understand what forgiveness means. Forgiveness is not a behavior, it does not mean the person who did something wrong will not be held accountable or that you are expected to interact with them. Rather, it means you learn to not carry the negativity implemented by that person upon you. To forgive, significant emotional work needs to be done. Forgiveness is a friend to the limbic system. Carrying deep internal anger and resentment toward someone will poison the limbic system.

Beside the emotional health and happiness of the brain, there are other areas of the brain that are responsible for feelings of peace, inner balance and equilibrium. For example, basal ganglia's role is to help us move and feel in balance and in response to the situation. Not overacting and not underacting. Problems with this area can create anxiety, tension, shakiness, headaches and low motivation. Techniques like guided imagery, a walk in nature, deep breathing and meditation can help with healing this part of the brain. Also, learning how to face and deal with conflict instead of avoiding and repressing it, what to eat to add to your sense of calmness rather than making you more anxious, and finding ways to take control of your over-reaction to situations can all help with this process.

In addition to what we discussed, the cingulate system which is responsible for attention and going from a thought to an action form can also be an important part of the brain when it comes to happiness and health. For example, having problems and imbalances in this area can cause people to feel stuck in a thought or behavior. Also, people who are constantly worried can have an imbalance in this area of the brain.

However, these are some of the example of how this unlimited potential we call the brain can affect us in everything we do, think, feel and interact with. The rest of the book will be focused on general aspects of the self and how each part of the brain may influence it.

The Spiritual Brain

What does a brain of a truly spiritual person looks like? What makes them feel spiritual? Different studies report a number of changes in the brain activity of a spiritual person. Before I move any further, I would like to define spirituality as a sense of inner content, inner peace, compassion, and universal empathy; a sense of connection to something deeper and more meaningful. It includes a thirst for self-discovery and learning about who you are and who you want to be, moving beyond your limits, healing yourself, making yourself to be your best possible self, connecting to others in a positive and healthy way, having a sense of direction, discipline (morality) and awareness.

Now that we've defined spirituality, let's discuss the spiritual brain. One report that caught my attention was that spiritual people have a sense of quieting of a small area in their brains - the right parietal lobe, which is more related to defining a "me". This is according to researcher Brick Johnstone of Missouri University. This area's activation is a necessity at the earlier developmental stage, as it gives us a sense of identity and foundation. This area is responsible for self-evaluation and self-control to be able to find our place in the world and to navigate it and relate with it. It is also the area that helps with us updating our self-awareness and self-discovery. However, once a person reaches a stage of enlightenment (complete self awareness and insight), this area's activation is not as needed, as the person naturally becomes what she was born to become. This profound spirituality is accompanied by less activation in this area of the brain. It is like the old saying that says when you chase a dream, after reaching it, don't get too attached to it.

At the stage in which the foundation for this "me" is built, the person needs to learn to let go of too much me-evaluation and just flow with life. This sense of selflessness focuses on a sense of internal liberation that highly spiritual people experience. This is the state where the person becomes more selfless, but to get there, the person has to follow the spiritual development stages. One cannot reach the top until she follows the stages; it is systematic, like a school system. The person at this stage realizes that they are one with their surroundings and what they do is affected and will affect the surrounding. At this level, the person's consciousness changes its dynamic and becomes a part of their being rather than just a thought process.

That is why damage to the spiritual part of the brain would not be a complete transcended state since the person cannot have this until they are fully actualized and have a complete sense of self. Only after forming this, they can move above it and become transcended.

Spiritual people who are as focused if not more on the world than themselves and care intensely about its matters tend to be more mentally, emotionally, physically and spiritually healthy.

Some techniques that can calm this self-evaluating side of the brain are spiritual/religion practices like meditation or prayer, learning ways to enjoy simple things of life through sensations, appreciating art and nature, and learning to connect more in-depth with diverse people.

A general map of the brain in relation to spirituality according to today's scientific research is as follows:

The God chemical is rooted in the brain stem.

The God spot is in the temporal lobe right above the brain stem.

The spiritual virtuosos is in the parietal lobe on the top left of the brain.

Near death experiences are experienced through the frontal lobe.

Now that we've discussed some of the areas of the brain related to spiritual sensations, let's move to the next part of this book, which is the emotional brain.

The Emotional Brain

The brain is a complex organ and science is discovering more and more about it. However, what we have so far is that there are three major parts to the brain going from the reptilian (at the base of the brain) to old mammalian (mid brain) to new mammalian (upper brain). The brain seems to be evolving and the more modern humans are using more of their upper brain than ever before. The reptilian brain is the seed to major emotions like fear and aggression, the old mammalian brain has the limbic system which controls general and more complex emotions, and the new mammalian brain uses reason and rationality to control the emotions in moderation, positively and productively. These change with learning, awareness, and experience. What makes us different from other species is that we can reason with our emotions and we can get better and better at this by increasing the activation of the frontal lobe.

One of the basic areas at the base of brain is called the amygdala. This area is responsible for the formation of a variety of basic emotions like affection, love, attachment, rage, aggression and fear.

This is the area responsible for the fight or flight response and forms ideas about information based on limited and quick processing. This is where you first decide if you like the person sitting next to you or not. The judgment of situations through the amygdala is emotional rather than rational, and while it is vital for the human brain to respond to certain situations quickly, in many other situations where rational judgment is necessary, the person has to train her mind to take the information to the new mammalian portion of the brain for processing before responding. For example, when the feeling or the thought of "I don't like this person" comes to mind; the information is then sent to the new mammalian part of the brain and you then analyze it to see if your judgment of this person is fair, based on something they did or your own way of cognition depending on your memories, emotions, and information. It's the same with when you like someone too much and too quickly. So, the amygdala is more related to the generation of emotions or planting the seed so to speak.

The other part of the brain is the hypothalamus, which is more connected to the generation of emotions and motivated actions like sex and hunger, which are also related to emotions. Some say that this structure may be related to extreme forms of rage and pleasure. The hippocampus helps a person remember the emotions that are related with past experiences.

Thalamus is another part of the emotional brain which is like a bridge. If the thalamus is damaged, it may affect the emotional part of the brain and the emotional response.

Then there is the frontal lobe area of the brain, which is a part of the new mammalian brain and deals with making rational choices, problem solving, impulse control and evaluating a situation; it is like the supervisor of all the rest. The frontal lobe is the part that allows a time lapse between feeling the emotion and responding to the emotion. The frontal lobe is a very complex system and the better developed it is, the more rational thinking and mature feelings the person will have. Rational thinking that is accompanied by a mature feeling creates actions and feelings like being fair, cooperative, unconditional love, compassion for all being, altruism, justice, harmony, beauty and peace.

Then, other emotional aspects of the brain may be affected by past memories. For example, a person who has been through deprivation or abuse as a child or any type of maltreatment may have problems with the brain's ability to process serotonin, which is the feel good neurotransmitter which helps with emotional stability. A brain developed in a confusing and non-nurturing environment that felt threatening puts the brain in a state of hyper alertness, focusing too much on strategies for survival even after the threat is removed. This is when the adult who has developed such tendencies does not seem to be able to function normally when he sees love, kindness, nurturing and positive stimulation. If the person is in a state of fear response, this intense and constant fear will drain the other parts of the brain that are needed for other functions. Such a person may also be experiencing a hyper arousal in which they have an altered baseline for arousal and overreact to situations that seem non-threatening.

In addition, such individuals, if they have experienced repeated abuse, may dissociate and mentally and emotionally remove themselves from a situation. This allows the individual to pretend nothing is wrong and while as a child in a threatening and abusive situation that may have worked well, as an adult and in situations where the person has to face reality and find solutions, this can be disabling. In other cases, the person, as a child, might have gone through abuse amnesia to sustain her attachment to the caregiver based on her survival needs, but then this amnestic memory of abuse may resurface and bring about flashbacks or nightmares.

When a person has had an upbringing in which they did not feel safe, calm, protected, and taken care of; such person's attachment style and the foundation for it may get damaged. Such a brain will focus more on day to day needs and survival rather than future growth, and if the person does not help themself heal from this, this brain pattern may continue into adulthood. Such an adult may have difficulties building deep relationships or may be very susceptible to stress. She may also have dependency tendencies and play the victim role in addition to not being able to put their emotions in check and in a balanced form. Such a person may also have lower growth in their hemisphere which affects tendencies for depression.

Now that we have discussed some areas of the emotional brain and the importance of brain work in order to be emotionally healthy, we can move on to the next chapter.

The Rational Brain

A rational brain is a brain that evaluates situations and tries to create positive results. It considers facts and what is available to come up with a solution. It is able to use critical thinking to solve problems. Critical thinking is important to filter out irrelevant information from the mind and only focus on what is important. A rational brain is not under the influence of media, peer pressure, culture or religion, but observes and learns what adds to the value of its contents. It does not act impulsively and analyses the situation before proceeding.

Someone whose brain is rational asks clear questions and does not accept things at face value. She looks beyond the tip of the iceberg and looks for the roots of a situation to find true reasons for an issue. As a result, a rational mind is less biased than a non-rational one.

A rational brain can control the emotions, balance them before responding, and use emotions as a great tool for gathering information and connecting to others and the surroundings. In addition, a brain that is rational has an easier time identifying a problem by looking at the facts of a situation and interpreting the situation in a way that is less contaminated.

Most anyone can increase their rational and logical functioning of the brain. The brain has plasticity, which means it can build new connections and renew its activity. This can be done by doing new and complex tasks and by stimulating the brain.

A brain that has strong cellular connection and cell density is one that can sustain its functionality for a longer period of time. A healthy and strong brain looks like a vivacious forest with many cellular connections. The brain needs moderate levels of variety, diversity and complexity to function at an optimal level.

When it comes to cognitive functioning and logical thinking, the brain has an unlimited capacity to take in information and to process it. The specific area of the brain that is related to thinking is the frontal lobe, which is one of the four areas of the cortex.

We share our more evolved brain, the rational brain, with other higher level mammals like dolphins, but we have the largest neocortex. The neocortex takes up about 2/3 of the human brain. The human brain has more capacity than any other species for doing tasks like abstract thinking, language development, becoming more and more conscious, and using imagination and intuition to create. This is why we are at the top of the food chain as a species. The neocortex has two sides, left and right, each called hemispheres. The right is more related to artistic, spatial and musical work while the left is more into the linear, rational and verbal work. But the two sides work hand in hand and affect each other's productivity.

The frontal lobe of the brain is the last part of the brain to develop, and this is the center of control. It also manages higher emotions like empathy, compassion and altruism. In addition, it is related to memory, concentration and attention, language, visual and spatial processing, and logic and reasoning.

To become a rational thinker learn to add knowledge to your mind, stimulate your mind to be curious, have an open but moderately skeptical mind, and learn to look beyond the tip of the iceberg. In addition, ask for the source of any information received, learn from experts who are trusted, have evidence for what you say, and make sure your mind does not get contaminated with confusing, corrupt, extreme and baseless information.

The Disciplined Brain

A disciplined brain is the brain of a person with self-control; in other words, people with self control have a more efficient brain. This effect is more correlational than causational meaning there is a relationship in which both can cause the other to increase or decrease.

In one specific study of the tempting marshmallows, which was first performed in the 1960s, asking 4-yr-old children to eat a marshmallow immediately or wait for 15 minutes and then get two, these children's level of self-control was measured. The follow up study indicated that the children who were able to hold out for the additional sweet grew up to be different from the ones who weren't able to do that. As teenagers, they received better SAT scores, were less likely to do drugs and alcohols, and as adults they were more physically fit, had more money in their bank account, and were less likely to get a divorce.

In addition, fMRI scanning of the brain of individuals with more self-control shows that in such individuals the brain network is used more directly and such individuals are able to find simple pathways to arrive to the answers at hand, while the lower self-control group uses an unnecessarily long pathway with more useless complexity. Furthermore, studies indicate that brains with the most efficient way of completing a task are able to exercise more self-control. In addition, there may be more activity in the frontal lobe of the brain of people who can control their impulses and delay their gratification when needed.

Self-control is the ability to control impulses and quick reactions. When used in moderation and wisely (common sense), it can become a vital tool for becoming internally liberated and giving the person a sense of self-empowerment. So, it is not at all limiting; on the other hand, in the long run it will actually be liberating. It is also important to have self-control if one wants to stay away from issues like obsession, irrational fear, addictions or any other type of destructive behavior or feeling.

To have more self-control, one must learn what it really means. Self-control has nothing to do with restricting yourself too much from what gives you pleasure. It just means you do cost benefit analysis in most situations to see if the benefits of your choices outweigh the cost, either for you or others, or if there is any short or long term damages that you need to consider. If there is harm, then self-control will give you the freedom to have a choice and to say no. So, remove the belief that self-control will limit your fun as this is an irrational belief with no evidence to support it.

To develop self-control, start with a list of priorities you want to have self-control towards. For example, do you want to eat healthy, do less impulsive shopping, do more work, read more, or quit smoking? After that try to see what emotions you have that are out of control - do you have too much anger, fear, aggression, jealously? Then check for what thoughts and beliefs bring about such negative feelings within you and start challenging those thoughts and beliefs. For example, do you have a fear of having pleasure? Then once you identify these, start writing a list of positive affirmations to practice and to re-shape your brain to become more disciplined.

Remember, you can be fully in control of yourself, your emotions don't run you but work for you, you have the power to change your thoughts and emotions if they do not work properly or don't make sense, you can have inner strength and success, you can be happy and have enjoyment in life, and you can act mature and get respect. And don't forget, you can have fun with self-control.

The Creative Brain

To learn to become creative, you have to let your brain get out of its own way and to learn to sometimes just go with the flow, be spontaneous and take responsible risks. While structure is an important task that the brain needs to learn, there has to be a balance between having a structure and being able to become spontaneous. When there is a sense of naturalness, the dorsolateral prefrontal and lateral orbital regions of the brain become less active and the medial prefrontal cortex, which is responsible for self-expression, becomes more active. At these moments of imprecision, the parts of the brain that are responsible for monitoring and evaluating behaviors quieten and let the creativity play its course. Here, more intuition and creativity is manifesting. In addition, the brain's sensory regions become more active during improvisation moments. Creativity is not really related solidly to any specific part of the brain, but rather letting the brain flow with different activities at different points.

As reported before, the brain has two different sides, the left and right hemispheres. It is as if these two have their own way of thinking. The left part of the brain is more analytical and logical while the right is more creative and emotional. But when it comes to true creativity, both of these sides should cooperate to create a piece that can be considered a unique addition to the work of art or a positive and productive expression. For example, Albert Einstein was very creative, but at the same time he was able to use the logical part of his brain to come up with ideas that were not only new but also relevant to the scientific community. At the end, the right side of the brain can be considered as an engine, but the left side is the one dealing with using this creativity to solve the problems of the world.

A few tips to becoming more creative are stimulating the brain by exercising it and having it solve problems.

Teach your brain to think differently, to learn new ways to act. For example, take a new route to work, date someone new, explore new places, learn a new task, and open up. In addition, experience life, meet new people, and diversify your life. Be open to different perspectives and try them if necessary. Remember, while you are making your brain better, reward it by acknowledging yourself.

To be a creative and logical person who creates positive things that contribute to this world, you have to learn to use your left brain's ability to think like a scientist, to want stability, to be able to categorize; to want to be accurate, linear, analytical and interested in strategies, and to want to be in control, to be a master of words, to be realistic, to be interested in order, logic and to have a sense of identity. But also, you want to have the right brain's ability to be creative, a free spirit, passionate, sensual, and playful, into movement, imagination and sensation.

The Intuitive Brain

Intuition is a form of brain process that happens automatically. A large portion of our mental processing happens without much conscious awareness and intuitively. Unconscious processes include emotional reactions to threat, implicit memory and subconscious perceptions, all of which shape our perception of reality and how we think, behave and respond to situations. Many times we may not be aware of them, but they are a part of us.

We have to approach intuition with the awareness that it is in some ways unconscious and rapid and that we have to be careful not to mix it up with simple guesswork.

Indeed, we specifically have to be careful with not fooling ourselves. But intuition is indeed a real and a powerful force.

Research indicates that human intelligence is much more than logic, thinking and ordering things, and that it also includes our social, spiritual, creative, intuitive, and emotional interactions.

Instinct and intuition go hand in hand and are this innate feeling toward a specific behavior or situation. These are not learned, they are innate. Some people call it a gut feeling, a hunch, a sensation that seems to come quickly into the consciousness without full awareness of the foundation and reasons behind it.

Not only do we need instinct, but we need it along with reason and logic to make the best decisions. So, we don't have to reject science to benefit from what an instinct has to offer as studies are now showing that the majority of brain's gray matter is related to the non-conscious thought rather than the conscious one.

In order to bring intuition back to our everyday life and learn how to make it work in parallel with our logic and reason, we have to learn to start a dialogue with it. We have to consider that while our conscious mind is working with logic our unconscious mind works with the past, present, and the future to create meaning in a nonlinear way. The unconscious would be the part that tells you to go for a hike when you are stuck with a project that is overly stressing you. The conscious part would be saying 'but I can't do it, it is too much'. The unconscious would say 'but the hiking and the break would relax you'. The conscious would say, 'what does relaxing have to do with what I am facing?' And the unconscious would respond, 'just do it and you will see, trust me'.

Maybe when you do take a break and relax, you will come up with ideas or a new form of energy to deal with the work at hand.

When you are working to bring more of your intuition out make sure that you keep a journal of your thoughts, that you turn off and quieten your inner judge who criticizes or analyzes things too much, and make sure you have private moments where you self-reflect and allow your emotions to flow freely. When you do these, you should be able to create a deeper connection with yourself and become more intuitive.

A Social Brain

Social connection is vital to human growth, happiness, and survival. A hurt feeling is created when a person feels lonely or rejected. This social hurt creating an emotional pain is related to a specific structure in the brain, the anterior cingulate cortex. This is the same area of the brain that also registers physical pain and maybe that is why in many senses the two pains are correlated.

Social interactions and having loving and supportive connections have been related to more health and happiness. People are different and some need more interaction and some less, but the foundation stays the same and that is the fact that healthy and positive interactions are vital to all of us. Studies indicate that neuropeptide oxytocin is the biochemical that carries the benefit of social interaction. This chemical plays a role in morality, social interaction, empathy, positive effect, and compassion.

Love has been identified by some researchers as not only an emotion but also a motivating force, a drive creating reward in the brain to seek specific stimuli. During a lifetime, for example when the person is experiencing romantic love; the brain's prefrontal cortex is collecting data and evaluating the situation to find the best possible way to achieve the sensation of love.

The process of social connection, love, and attachment can also be hurtful. For example, people can suffer from severe depression when they feel rejected.

Love has different categories, from lust to attraction to attachment. Lust is more related to a form of sexual attraction and is associated with androgens and estrogens. Attraction can be more of a feeling of passion along with the mood-swings associated with the state of the attraction, then the thought process associated with the object of attraction and all of these are related to high dopamine and norepinephrine and low serotonin. Then the healthy attachment part of love, which brings about a sense of calm and inner peace, security, stability and long term commitment, is associated with the hormones oxytocin and vasopressin. So, it may start from lust but if there is more to it, it will go toward an intimate attraction and then a form of healthy attachment.

As love changes from, so does the brain's chemistry, so as attachment replaces lust and passion, high levels of oxytocin and vasopressin start interfering with dopamine and norepinephrine.

Other things interfering with this process include high levels of testosterone. High levels of this hormone tend to suppress oxytocin and vasopressin. Evidence indicate that men who have high levels of testosterone tend to be more controlling, have less long term relationships, and more divorces.

A few other findings indicate that high dopamine and norepinephrine may lower the chances of experiencing romantic love. On the other hand, low serotonin is related to romantic love, obsessive thinking, and intense sexual attraction. The kind of obsessive thoughts these romantic subjects go through is similar to OCD, which is also affected by low levels of serotonin.

Relationships shape the circuitry of the brain, memory, emotion, and self-awareness.

The brain is extremely flexible and capable of changing; it is best functioning where placed in a joy and discovery mode which comes with interaction with others. We are inner dependent with others for our growth and this inner dependency does not stop with age. By resolving conflicts, building healthy connections, giving and receiving love, giving and receiving support and encouragement, and giving and receiving information and awareness, we are stimulating our brain and its development. Moderate levels of challenges, the ones that do not create an overwhelming sense of stress, can actually be good and stimulating to the growth of new brain cells, whereas challenges that create unbearable stress can have the opposite effect. So, that is why it is better to get away from abusive, neglectful and draining interactions.

And finally some quick tips to work on building healthy relationships include being yourself and allowing others to do the same, not being judgmental, working on learning to have open/respectful/honest communication skills, learning how to give love and appreciation and how to receive it, knowing how to be silly at times and take it easy, learning to find humor in things and not to take it too seriously while finding a solution to the problem, taking time to socialize and build connections, not taking the caring side of people for granted, learning to attract positives, and having boundaries with the negatives.

A Balanced Brain

A balanced brain is creative, a deep thinker, intuitive, and rational; it also performs well, feels fulfilled, connects well with others, does not over or under react to situations and is a generally happy brain, all the while being capable of feeling temporary pain that is proportionate to the situation. A healthy brain creates healthy behaviors, healthy feelings, and healthy thoughts. In addition, a healthy brain is free from internal and unnecessary external conflicts.

When a brain is balanced and healthy, the person feels a sense of wellbeing despite what is going on around her. She can cope with life's challenges better and can bounce back easier from adversity; she is also more capable of enjoying life's many offers.

A balanced brain is also capable of understanding how to use the unlimited external information and stimulation and how much of them to use for managing life effectively. In addition, it thinks about ideas and possibilities that an unhealthy brain is incapable of doing.

Nowadays, brain technology can be used to help people free themselves from many type of constraints and limitations. This technology can show people where the brain is out of balance and not functioning well and how to fix it or cope with it. The brain has an amazing capacity to heal and readjust itself. As the brain balances and heals and stabilizes itself, the person becomes emotionally more intelligent, mentally clearer, and socially and spiritually more advanced and more evolved. Such a person will also by physically healthier. When anger, insecurity, anxiety, regret, guilt, shame, aggression, fear, depression, helplessness are releases, or when the need for alcohol and drug use and impulsivity are removed and are replaced with positivity, balance, content, compassion, peace, and rationality, the world starts opening up to you.

Balance has two parts to it – the brain's relationship with the external world and its relationship with the internal world. The external world is things like work, profession, education, relationships, hobbies, interests, creative pursuits and things of that nature; the internal world would be things like self-reflection, self-evaluation, self-improvement, and focusing on your heart and mind.

A balanced and fully functioning brain has proportionate functioning in its intuitive thinking, logical thinking, and creativity. When we have a whole brain in use, we can think in a linear and sequential way, taking each part of information and looking at it systematically, and will be able to plan and achieve specific goals. However, it will also have a nonlinear and holistic way of processing information where things are looked at from the bigger picture. Such a person is not only focused on facts, reality and logic, but also is open to the mystical and spiritual experiences of life. In addition, such a person is easily able to adopt and follow rules, but at the same can help change rules if they are unfit, irrational or unjust.

A fully functioning brain acknowledges the reality as it is and does not deny it. If there is an area that needs to be addressed, a fully functioning mind does that. It does not neglect what needs attention and does not attend too much to what is not needed. In addition, it is capable of evaluating life, setting reasonable goals, planning, reflecting, preparing, connecting, self-empowering, and opening up.

Last Words

As we want to become a complete or a fully functioning human being, what some call evolve, self-actu-
alized or something else, we need to make sure our brain,
which the device through which we experience our self
and our life, is functioning properly and in balance. This
book discussed some of the general explanations of how
each part of the brain shapes who we are and how we
can work on it to make it a more balanced brain. When
we have a balanced and healthy brain, we are mentally,
spiritually and socially healthy.

The characteristics of a mentally healthy person includes
a positive and valid sense of self concepts, ability to look

at things positively but be aware of what is not working, having a sense of responsibility for one's life, having healthy connections, being flexible and adaptable, being able to accept necessary change, being able to face problems with a calm mind, and being open minded and willing to ask for constructive criticism.

A person who is spiritually healthy is humble but has boundaries, can say yes or no to situations, is honest and authentic, does not discriminate and does not hold on to negative views of people based on the surface, is involved with doing something good for the world, is fair and just in their interactions with others, is rationally and emotionally mature, and has found a bridge between the two.

A person who is psychologically healthy is moderately open to life, meaning while such a person has a solid structure, base, and foundation, they are willing to explore life with open arms. Such a person changes what they can, accepts what they cannot change, and is aware of the difference between the two. They are also willing to take responsibility and sensible risks. A psychologically healthy person is also conscious to where they are disciplined, has high moral values and follows the ethical rules, but at the same time are not too attached to their discipline and can challenge moral and ethical rules if they are outdated, unjust for the greater good, and do not make any sense to their growth. In addition, a person who is psychologically healthy is a combination of an extrovert and an introvert, meaning not only do they enjoy spending time with others, socializing and getting out there, but also spend time alone reflecting, recharging and re-focusing on what is really important and gaining an appreciative perspective in life. Such a person is also capable of trust but not a blind form of trust; they have a basic level of regard for everyone but are also aware of the fact that they have to have clear boundaries in their interactions with people to lessen conflict, confusion, and unnecessary drama or hurt. Such a person protects their health, self-esteem and wellbeing, and respects that in others. And last but not least, a psychologically healthy individual does not hold on to negative emotions, does not get easily frustrated with things, does not have feelings of hate, aggression, or jealousy. To get there, one needs to do some deep work, but everyone is capable of doing it. The first step is walking out of the denial and stopping trying to pretend to be what one isn't.

About the Author

Dr. Roya Rohani Rad's educational background is in Psychology. She holds a Master's degree in Applied Psychology and an APA accredited Doctorate degree in  Clinical Psychology. She is a teacher, an artist, and a writer. Dr. Rad's books and writings focus on the subjects of self-actualization, spirituality, self-growth, brain, healthy living, healthy relationships, culture, identity and many more. She also writes poetry. Dr. Rad's writings focus on quality and she attempts to put as much information in as few pages as she possibly can. Her books are typically longer than an article and shorter than a typical book.

More information can be found on her website www.SelfKnowledgeBase.com

A Word from the Author

For quite some time now, I have been interested in the concepts of spirituality, psychology and self-growth. I wanted to find a way to make these work together to explain a more comprehensive way of living and being. In addition, I wanted to see how I can find a bridge between these to make them more complete and applicable to this fast pacing and complex world.

My writing style is focused on the type of material that is easy to comprehend and up to the point. I know many people in today's world are busy and are usually multi-tasking and my intention ***is to put as much reliable information into as few pages as possible***. I also allow limited editing to my work to make sure my thoughts are communicated to my readers as intended. My hope is to encourage my readers to realize that there is a power within them that they can unleash through increasing their awareness, gaining more knowledge, learning to be content, experiencing life, and having a sense of true faith (not a blind one). I hope to do this through teaching my readers that the relationship between their mind and body and all the many layers of them is unbeatable and that they need to learn how this fascinating system works to have access to their free will. Free will, to me, is something that we all have access to but not that many of us know how to gain access to it. Sometimes, we become slaves to our mind, our surrounding, and our own addictive behaviors and cannot see what lies right in front of us.

My work also encourages people to know that they need to:

Acknowledge their past to learn from it but we cannot get stuck to it.

To cut the cord to any negativity and find peace with our life without denying or repressing what we need to focus on.

Learn to train our mind and our heart to focus on the present, learning how to be content with what life has to offer.

Have reasonable goals and plans for the future, planning the seed to make sure we sustain a healthy, secure, and peaceful life and to make sure we are a productive member of this world who adds something positive to it.

Realize that we are perfect only when we are aware of our shadow side and our shortcomings as human beings and that the more we are aware, the less these shortcomings and our shadow will be in control of our destiny.

<u>Other Books By Dr.Rad</u> (for more information about these books and the upcoming ones and how to get a copy check www.SelfKnowledgeBase.com)

<u>Marriage: till shit do us part</u>

A comprehensive but yet simple and up to the point book that can help those of you who truly want to save your marriage or your relationship. While there are some relationships that must end due to their shaky foundation and complete incompatibility but the majority of them can be saved. This book helps you choose the right relationship when you're ready, sustain your relationship, and make it work so it would benefit you and your partner. It also shows you some of the unconscious patterns that influence you when choosing a mate. Yet another subject of this book is differentiating an empty and shallow relationship from a fulfilling and complete one. While not a destination but definitely a process that you can work on. Author: Dr. Roya R. Rad, MA, PsyD. **copyright** © 2012 Roya R Rad

Guides

A series of spiritual, intuitive, inspirational and motivational phrases. This book points to the fact that for a complete sense of self, it is important and vital to have both an aware mind and a pure heart. The first comes through cognitive modification and an increasing awareness and understanding through learning and life's diverse experiences. The second comes through working with the emotional self, balancing you're out of balance feelings, and working through any blockages. Author: Dr. Roya R Rad, MA, PsyD. **copyright** © 2012 Roya R Rad

Where Is My Place In This World

This book focuses on differentiating the higher self from the lower one. In addition, it explains the characteristics of each and how to train your mind to become more logical and your heart to get rid of the toxins and become pure. After that work is done, you can find a bridge between your mind and your heart and function from a complete self and start the process of growth from there. We come to this world selfless but yet immature. We go through the process of life, forming an identity, becoming conditioned in order to learn and expand. But then after accomplishing all those goals, we need to again get to a place where we let go of these and become selfless again. But there is a difference, this stage of selflessness is a mature and solid one since it now comes with awareness. Therefore, there is a "me" that is now functioning from a place of unity with others where there is tolerance, rationality, compassion, accountability, and an unconditional love. Author: Dr. Roya R. Rad, MA, PsyD. **copyright** © 2010 Roya R Rad

Rumi & Self Psychology

Two astonishing perspectives of the art and science of self-transformation: Rumi's poetic language vs. Carl Jung's language of psychology. Author: Dr. Roya R. Rad, MA, PsyD. **copyright** © 2007 Roya R Rad

Psyche and self's theories in psychology

Comparing and simplifying a number of theories about personality including Carl Jung and Maslow. Authro: Dr. Roya R. Rad, MA, PsyD. **copyright** © 2010 Roya R Rad